Between Silence And Scream

Varsha Viswaprakash

BookLeaf Publishing

India | USA | UK

Made with ❤ on the BookLeaf Publishing Platform
www.bookleafpub.in
www.bookleafpub.com

Dedication

To the dreamers and the seekers,
Who wander through the labyrinth of thought,
Gathering the scattered pieces of their imagination.
These fragments of thought have made me who I am
today,
And they will continue to shape me until the day I
disappear from this world.

I want all of you who read this book to understand:
We are what we think.
Embrace your thoughts,
For they are the essence of who you are.

May you find beauty in the fragments,
And strength in the stories they tell.
This work is for you-
In every moment of reflection,
Every spark of inspiration,
And every whisper of the heart.

Preface

In the quiet corners of our minds, thoughts drift like scattered leaves on a breeze—some vivid and bright, others faded and distant. Each fragment holds a piece of our story, shaping who we are and how we perceive the world around us. This book, *Between Silence and Scream*, is a collection of those thoughts, a journey through the intricate tapestry of consciousness that defines our existence.

As I reflected on my own experiences, I realized that every thought, no matter how fleeting, contributes to the essence of our being. From moments of joy and clarity to times of confusion and doubt, these fragments have guided me, challenged me, and ultimately defined me. Each chapter unfolds like a conversation with oneself, encouraging you to delve deep into your own mind. It's an invitation to embrace the power of your thoughts, to recognize that they shape not only your perception but also your reality. We are what we think, and by embracing our innermost reflections, we can uncover the truths that reside within us.

As you turn the pages, I encourage you to ponder your own fragments. What thoughts have shaped your journey? What stories lie hidden beneath the surface? Together, let's navigate this landscape of the mind, celebrating the beauty of our unique experiences and the connections that bind us.

Thank you for joining me on this voyage. May you find inspiration, solace, and perhaps even a piece of yourself within these pages.

Acknowledgements

In true acknowledgment of the thoughts that have developed in my mind, I want to thank myself for facing all the challenges and striving to be a better version of myself every day. This journey is not just mine; it belongs to all of us.

I extend my gratitude to my parents, teachers, friends, and family, with a special mention of my grandmother, my aunt, and my grandfathers in heaven. May you rest in peace. I hope to make you proud every day and to achieve everything you aspired to in your own lives, fulfilling the dreams you left behind. Last but not least, I want to thank God Almighty, my protector and my all, who has been there for me when no one else was. Amen.

1. When Was the Last Time?

Do you remember the last time
you were excited about crayons?
The last time the world of cartoons
filled you with wonder?
The last time the swing set
sent you soaring into the sky?
I don't.

Sometimes, it feels like we never truly realize
when one phase of life is ending.
I can't recall the last day
I decided, "This is it."
The day I stopped watching cartoons,
stopped believing in Santa Claus,
or let go of my coloring books.
It all fades into the background.

Today, as I look back,
I see that I never noticed
the moment I stepped into my teenage years,

or the day I crossed into adulthood.
Everything around me stayed still,
but my interests shifted,
like the seasons changing,
unnoticed until it's too late.

Life isn't always comforting.
It can be a gentle reminder
that as we grow,
some joys slip away,
and new ones await,
hidden in the shadows
of our changing selves.

2. Today years old

Today will be the oldest you have ever been
and the youngest you will ever be.
I stumbled upon this thought,
and it reverberated through my mind-
how much weight lies in those few words,
how many layers of meaning
have been wrapped in their simplicity.

It's okay to stumble, to falter,
for each day is your first day
of adulthood,
a delicate dance of uncertainty
where mistakes are merely steps
on the path to growth.
Let the echoes of laughter,
the scent of morning coffee,
and the warmth of fleeting moments
fill your spirit,
for today is a treasure you'll never relive.

Look closely:
your skin holds stories,
your hair whispers of time passing,
your body reflects change—
all indications that you are not
the same as you were yesterday.
Each sunrise invites you to redefine
what it means to live,
to savor the small wonders
that often slip by unnoticed.

Today is a singular thread,
a fleeting heartbeat in the vast expanse.
"Kal ho, na hoo"-
tomorrow may or may not happen.
So embrace this moment,
this paradox of age and youth,
and allow it to awaken a deeper appreciation
for the life unfolding around you.
Pause, reflect, and let it linger,
for today is not just a day;
it is a profound gift.

3. Figuring out Adulthood

In the shadow of adulthood,
where the cake is sweet but stale,
birthdays pass like whispered dreams,
each day a thread in an unraveling fabric.
Am I alone in this vast expanse,
where longing clings like dew on morning grass?

Once you lace up those grown-up shoes,
the world narrows to a path unyielding
the laughter of youth fades,
replaced by the sighs of obligation.
Stressed, I wander this landscape,
neither sad nor happy,
a traveler lost in the fog of routine.

I long for the simplicity of nature,
to roam barefoot on fertile soil,
to savor sun-ripened fruits,
to dive into the cool embrace of rivers,
where God's creation breathes and sings,

unfettered by the weight of deadlines.

When will I witness the wild?
The mountains that cradle the sky,
the forests that murmur ancient secrets?
I ache for that connection,
for the feminine spirit within,
for the dance of freedom
that once filled my soul.

Oh, God, save our weary generation
lead us back to the earth,
where we can breathe deeply,
and discover what it means to simply... be.

4. In Her Absence

In the depths of my heart, a sorrow does abide,
For the one who once stood steadfast by my side.
Oh, how I long for her presence, a sweet refrain,
She held my hand when shadows cloaked my pain.

When storms did rage and thunder gripped the night,
She drew me close, a beacon, soft and bright.
With whispers of courage, she taught me to stand,
Her wisdom a melody, like an old, cherished band.

In tempestuous moments, her laughter would play,
A balm for my fury, she'd ease it away.
A fragment of me, entwined in her grace,
A love so profound, none could replace.

Yet cruel fate's hand dealt its sorrowful blow,
Leaving echoes of love where heartaches grow.
The pain of farewell, the sharpest of blades,
Each day without her, a memory fades.

Still, she lives within me, coursing through my veins,
Her spirit, a whisper that forever remains.
In the rhythm of heartbeats, her essence I find,
A love that transcends, unbound by the mind.

Forever I carry her, deep in my soul,
Her influence shaping the woman I know.
Grateful am I for the light she bestowed,
For in her embrace, my true self has glowed.

In the depths of my heart, your memory will chime,
Though you've departed, your love transcends time.
A bond unbreakable, an eternal flame,
In the quiet of absence, I whisper your name.

5. Beyond the Rope

With tears blurred in the tapestry of my thoughts,
I recall the laughter that cut through the air,
A fellow soul, mocking my struggle,
As if my worth could be measured by a rope.

In the grip of challenge, I poured out my heart,
Pushing through pain, even in those days of crimson,
Scars traced my body, a map of my efforts,
Each failure a lesson, each tear a testament.

I remember the moments, suspended in doubt,
Crying on the line, where strength faltered,
Yet admiration swelled for those who soared,
For I knew in my heart, their triumphs were real.

Now, as a surveyor, I tread my own path,
Respecting the skill that others command,
For not every challenge fits every frame,
And kindness is the compass that guides us all.

I think of that man, still finding his way,
At twenty-seven, grappling with his own doubts,
But I choose silence, for not every voice deserves,
An explanation of my worth, my journey, my scars.

In the end, we are more than the ropes we climb,
More than the laughter that seeks to belittle,
We are the strength in our struggles, the grace in our
falls,
And the kindness we offer, understanding that we all-
Are navigating our own tangled paths,
With the courage to rise, despite the weight of the world.

6. The Gentle Women

In this wild age, where emotions spin,
A woman bears her burdens, thick as sin.
With shoulders stooped beneath a weight unseen,
No gallant knight to lift her from routine.

Where has the grace of kindness flown,
The tender touch that once was gently sown?
In shadows of a world that's lost its way,
The feminine heart learns to forge and fray.

Yet deep within, a spark of hope remains,
A longing for the gentle, sweet refrains.
To be a lady-yes, a cherished role,
Where strength can rest, and softness makes us whole.

But pause now, gentlemen, and look around,
Before you push that door to solid ground.
If there's a lady there, let her go first,
A simple act of honor-quench the thirst.

Open the door to her car, a grace,
She knows the way; it's not a daunting race.
Yet offer it, for she's a treasure rare,
Not weak, but strong; your kindness shows you care.

You're not obliged, but rather, take this cue-
How men are raised reflects in all you do.
In this modern dance, let kindness lead,
And weave a world where every heart is freed.

For this generation, with its heavy sighs,
Must learn again to see through softer eyes.
To honor all, to lift the weight we share,
And cultivate a world where kindness fills the air.

7. Tears of Power

In a foreign land, I rise with the sun,
Each day a march, a silent run–
To work, to toil, then back to a hollow space,
An empty home, a weary embrace.

For a year I circle this lonely track,
Dreaming of home, but the clock holds me back.
What others call luxury, I call bittersweet,
For in the stillness, my heart feels the heat.

When will I gather with loved ones near?
When will laughter fill the air, crystal clear?
When will I share a cup of tea, warm and true,
With friends who remember the essence of you?

These questions weigh heavy, each day I endure,
As riches and status seem less than secure.
Life isn't measured by coins in a chest;
It's the moments we treasure, the times we feel blessed.

We labor for honor, for pride in their eyes,
But is it worth trading the joy for the prize?
Time is the currency, not merely the gold,
In memories woven, our stories unfold.

So I gather my tears, each drop filled with fire,
A testament to longing, to love, and desire.
Let's lift up our voices, let our spirits soar,
For life is a journey, rich at its core.

In the heart of the struggle, let's find our way,
To cherish the now, not just live for the day.
Embrace every moment, let time be your guide-
For in love and connection, true wealth does abide.

8. Is it Love?

Is it love, when I place another before my own frail
heart?
Is it love, when their laughter becomes the balm to my
weary soul?
Is it love, when I seek to shield them from the tempests
I've endured,
Warding off shadows that loom in the recesses of my
memory?

Is it love, when I don a mask of cheerfulness,
Concealing my tribulations beneath a veneer of
gratitude,
Cherishing their presence while my own burdens remain
unspoken?
These enigmas, a mosaic of bittersweet longing.

I loved my parents first,
Falling for them as one might fall for the dawn,
Twenty-three years woven in a fabric of unwavering
devotion,

A bond tempered in the crucible of time's relentless
passage.

In youth's fervor, friendships ignited like celestial bodies,
And infatuations flitted like ephemeral fireflies,
Yet, the essence of true love eluded my grasp,
Until the threshold of adulthood beckoned me inward,
Whispering tenderly to my own spirit, "I love you,"
Choosing to embrace the sanctuary of self.

Now, my parents remain my lodestar,
Their love, the fertile soil from which I blossom,
And my grandparents, a cherished lineage of warmth,
Their affection enveloping me in a cocoon of solace.

Life unfolds as a spiraling sonnet, an eternal refrain,
And we are oft left to ponder whom we hold dearest.
I yearn for a conduit to disclose this profound depth,
To lay bare the spectrum of my ardor,
To manifest how love weaves through the fabric of
existence,
Binding us in an intricate web of shared experience.

In this delicate ballet of affection, let us venerate one
another,
For love transcends mere emotion; it is the choice we
espouse,

A reflection of the beauty we perceive in each other,
An ever-evolving narrative inscribed upon the
parchment of our souls.

9. On the Perils of Time Misplaced

In days of yore, when hearts entwined did glow,
Behold the plight of souls who seek the light-
The fleeting hours, mere shadows on the flow,
Yet oft, excuse prevails, a wretched sight.

For he who claims he cannot find the time,
In truth, seeks but the company of few;
With those whose hearts are bound in passions prime,
While casting you aside, as winds oft do.

O waste not thy sweet hours on fickle kin,
For they who do not cherish what you give
Shall turn their backs, and thus your joys grow thin;
Remember this, and in thyself, believe.

Take not thy key of happiness, I say,
And grant it not to those who cannot see
The worth of kindness in a world of gray-
Keep it within, where it shall ever be.

Be gentle still, yet guard thy heart's domain,
For kindness may invite the sharpest thorn;
This world, unkind, oft treats the meek with disdain-
Let not thy spirit by their scorn be worn.

Thus, when you seek the warmth of friendship true,
Reflect on those who treasure what you bring;
For time is gold, and should be spent with few
Who honor thee, and to thy heart take wing.

10. I Will Find My Way

I have worn the weight of others' shoes,
A doormat, trampled, tossed aside
Discarded when my softness proves
Too meek for those who take, who bide.

In moments dark, I raise my hands to skies,
Where shadows linger, seeking light divine;
For in the stillness, I hear whispered sighs
A promise: I am mine, and I am fine.

Too often I've extended warmth to frost,
Kindness given where it's coldly scorned.
I will not wait for approval, nor be lost
In others' whispers, or their scorn, adorned.

Your worth is not a topic for their talk;
Time slips like sand through a clenched, tired fist.
Live not for judgments as the clocks tick-tock,
But remain true to the soul they've missed.

This world is not a mirror of our deeds;
It bends and twists, a dance of unfair sway.
Let them be shadows; I'll grow from my seeds-
In my own light, I'll find my way.

11. The Guiding Stars

This is for you, my steadfast guides,
Whose love has shaped my every stride.
In your embrace, I learned to soar,
The finest teachers, and so much more.

With laughter bright and tears that flow,
You opened worlds I longed to know.
In honesty, my heart found home,
No need to hide, no fear to roam.

As I step forth into this new dawn,
I glance at peers, yet feel not forlorn
For in your care, I've grown so wise,
Grateful for the gift of your eyes.

In youth, I chafed at rules you laid,
No phones, no screens, a choice I weighed.
Yet now, in quiet reflection, I see
The wisdom woven into your decree.

You are the roots that ground my soul,
My constant light, my cherished whole.
Forever in me, your spirits reside,
In every heartbeat, you are my guide.

What greater blessing could I desire
Than to be your daughter, to light the fire?
In every life, I'd choose you anew,
No change, no doubt, my heart beats true.

And in a future where time unwinds,
I wish for roles where our love entwines-
To hold you close as my dear children,
To shower you with love, unhidden.

In this sacred bond, I vow to stay,
My love for you will never fray.
For in the magic of life we weave,
You are my heart; I shall never leave.

12. Whispers of Sacrifice

Today, as the sun dipped low,
I wandered the beach where dreams ebb and flow.
Expats, lost in thought, traced their futures in sand,
Yearning for families, with distant hearts fanned.

Among them, a maid on a weathered bench sat,
Tending a child while the parents fell flat,
Unseen, unacknowledged, the love they neglect-
What weight will this child carry, what heart will reflect?

Innocence glimmered in the eyes of the young,
Yet the warmth of his nanny was the song he had sung.
But beside her, another boy, sadness etched in his face,
Longing for affection in this heart-wrenching space.

"Why won't they share?" he whispered, forlorn,
While his mother, so weary, wore the mantle of scorn.
A helpless love stretched thin like the evening's last
light,
Her heart split in two, as shadows engulfed night.

Life's canvas is cruel, painted shades of despair,
Yet I believe in the strength born from love that we
share.
This maid's child, though burdened, will rise through the
strife,
Emerging from shadows, crafting his own life.

May the tides guide him gently, through struggles he'll
grow,
Into something resilient, with a radiant glow.
For amidst the unfairness, hope flickers and sings,
In the hearts of the weary, true strength always springs.

13. In the Light of Being

Who can inspire me more than my own heart?
In a world where companions become rivals, torn apart.
Everyone's racing, forgetting to breathe,
In the shadows of competition, it's hard to believe.

Some days, the weight feels too heavy to bear,
Caught in a loop, in a game that's unfair.
I long for a circle where kindness reigns,
Where we lift each other, not bound by the chains.

Why must we exist in this endless race,
Where value is measured by a winner's embrace?
What's wrong with celebrating the gifts we possess,
Instead of striving to prove we are better, no less?

God crafted us uniquely, each with our own song,
Embrace your own journey; it's where you belong.
On days when the shadows pull me from light,
I remember I'm meant to rise, to shine bright.

For the world needs my presence, my voice, and my
grace,
To walk through the struggles, to find my own space.
So I'll stand up, though weary, with purpose anew,
For in being myself, I'll inspire others too.

14. Melody in Melancholy

How can I not speak of you, my silent guide?
On days when shadows linger, you're always by my side.
When hope seems fleeting, and the world feels cold,
You're the whisper in my heart, the warmth I hold.

In moments of doubt, when I falter and sway,
You cradle my spirit, turning night into day.
Once, lost in thought, I trudged through my fears,
And a child's gentle words washed away my tears:
"You look beautiful," they said, and in that fleeting
glance,
The universe shifted, as if I'd been given a chance.

You appear in the laughter, in kindness bestowed,
In the simplest of moments, your love is bestowed.
I connect with you, like magic that flows,
Through every blessing, my gratitude grows.

Oh, how can I thank you for this life I now see?
For the strength you've instilled, for setting me free.

Without you, dear God, who would I even be?
In loneliness and struggle, you've held me gently.

I never questioned the trials or pain,
Instead, I believed in the wisdom you gain.
You hold me close in the darkness of night,
And I walk in your blessings, bathed in your light.

With each passing moment, I cherish and adore,
For in every heartbeat, I find you once more.
You are the essence of who I aspire to be,
My beloved God, my heart sings in unity.

15. The Sweetest Little Treasure

Hey there, never lose the child in you
Hold tight to laughter, to wonder so true.
Make mistakes, let curiosity roam,
It's in these small joys that life finds its home.

Cast aside the whispers of doubt and disdain,
Don't seek their approval; let your spirit remain.
Be as optimistic as you once were,
Embrace each moment, let your heart stir.

I've walked through shadows, faced trials of old,
Yet I yearn for that childhood, vibrant and bold.
I cherish the little one I'm raising with care,
For in her joy, my own heart learns to flare.

I don't need others to treat me like small,
But I'll revel in each little wonder, embracing them all.
From ladybugs dancing to bicycle rides,
These simple delights fill my heart with pride.

So keep this flame bright, let it never dim-
For life's sweetest treasures lie within.

16. First Love

Does your first have to be your last?
First love sparkles, a tender thrill-
It's that first rush, the heartbeat that feels real.
But perfection? No, that's a myth we chase.

Think of the first smile, the wobbly steps,
The words we fumbled, the lessons in depth.
Not every beginning is flawless or bright,
Each misstep just shapes us, guides us toward light.

Hold tight to your vibe; let your spirit be free,
The one meant for you will come eventually.
Those who don't linger might show you the way,
Leading to love that's destined to stay.

And yes, the first will always hold a place-
In your heart's gallery, it wears a soft grace.
So cherish that feeling, let it live on,
For first loves are treasures that never are gone.

17. The Tight Chain

Shake off the weight of what others say,
Their negativity just pulls you away.
You don't need their doubts to hold you back
Rise up, think like royalty, get back on track.

It's all about mindset; that's where it starts,
When you believe in yourself, you'll play all your parts.
Let their voices fade; you're meant to shine,
Embrace your own power; make your path divine.

Unstoppable is more than a catchphrase or dream
It's about owning your journey, finding your theme.
So take a deep breath, let go of the noise,
In the silence of your heart, rediscover your voice.

You're the author of your story, let it unfold,
With each step you take, be brave and be bold.
The world's waiting for you, so step into the light
Free yourself from their weight, and take flight.

18. To the Single Born Ones

To the single born ones, let's speak the truth,
They say you're lucky, but they miss the proof.
No need to share, no limits on toys,
Yet in silent rooms, you'll hear your own voice.

The days spent alone, where toys were your friends,
Imagined conversations that never quite end.
With both parents busy, your heart felt the ache,
As the clock ticked slowly, a longing to break.

"Why do you enjoy your own company?" they ask,
But they don't see the layers behind this mask.
You learned to wait patiently for love's sweet embrace,
While others had siblings, you found your own space.

In a world filled with laughter, you stood on the side,
Wishing for someone to be there as a guide.
Loneliness, they say, is a shadow of luck,
But for those who've lived it, it's a heavy weight to
pluck.

We talk to ourselves; we're our own best friends,
In a journey of strength that never quite ends.
The toughest moments shape the heart's true core,
Each trial faced alone, it's a warrior's lore.

I watched as they played, those children so near,
Wishing for connection, for someone to hear.
Cousins would gather, sharing laughter and tears,
While I felt the void, my heart full of fears.

What if I stumble? Who's there to support?
In a world full of pairs, I felt like a fort.
So I stayed home often, avoiding the crowd,
In a silent rebellion, my heart wrapped in shrouds.

Being single born isn't a charm to behold,
It's a path marked with courage, a story untold.
Yet in the solitude, I've found strength to arise,
For the child within learns to dream and to fly.

So to all the single born, know this to be true:
You're resilient, you're vibrant, your heart's deep and
blue.
Embrace your own journey, the struggles you face,
For in the quiet moments, you'll find your own grace.

19. Letting Go

The moment they learned you would come,
How their hearts swelled with joy,
How they celebrated, the sweets they'd share,
Their firstborn, a dream realized?

You are not less valued; never doubt this truth,
From the very start, you were their angel,
Held close in love's embrace,
A precious light in their lives.

Respect that bond, for it runs deep,
Do not cast aside their care,
You are meant to honor them,
As they once cradled your fragile heart.

If they stumbled, if their joy was brief,
Forgive them, for they too were new,
Navigating the path of parenthood,
Learning as they went, just as you do.

Let us heal the wounds of our past,
Embrace them for who they are,
For perhaps they too, in their youth,
Longed for love, a gentle touch,
That could have changed their way.

So care for them now, in every way,
For love is a circle, a sacred return,
Think deeply on this, let kindness flow,
In understanding, we learn to grow.

20. Reflections

The moon ascends in the velvet sky,
As birds flit homeward, their calls a sigh.
Footfalls quicken, the world in a rush,
While shadows linger, in the evening's hush.

Neighbors gather, laughter mingles with wine,
Yet here I sit, lost in thoughts of mine.
A roadside watcher, I ponder the night,
Amidst the joy, I dwell in twilight's light.

In this solitude, the stars softly gleam,
Whispering secrets, cradling a dream.
Though others find warmth in the hearth's gentle glow,
I find my solace in the moon's silver flow.

21. Promises of Tomorrow

Death is a truth we all must face,
A shadow woven through time and space.
Yet when it strikes a heart so near,
The world unravels, and all feels unclear.

Laughter dims, the silence grows loud,
An empty chair where warmth once was proud.
Life's unpredictable, a winding path,
Where joy and sorrow share their aftermath.

Home grows quiet, echoes softly fade,
In the weight of loss, our hopes are laid.
Fairness can falter, like leaves in the breeze,
Yet in the stillness, we learn to find peace.

Let us promise them, in whispers of night,
To be born again, in a future so bright.
To hug a bit tighter, in each life we embrace,
To linger in love, in time and in space.

To cherish the moments, both big and small,
To hold onto laughter, to rise after the fall.
In every reunion, in each shared delight,
We weave our connection, through day and through
night.

In the depth of sorrow, we gather our might,
Holding the memories that flicker like light.
For love lingers on, in each whispered thought,
A bond that endures, no matter the cost.

And when shadows gather, as they sometimes will,
We'll find strength in promise, our hearts to fulfill.
Together we'll journey, through every endeavor,
Bound by the love that shall last forever.